The Coolest Pets

Reptiles and Amphibians

Anne O'Daly

KidHaven
PUBLISHING

Published in 2024 by
KidHaven Publishing, an Imprint of Greenhaven Publishing, LLC
2544 Clinton St., Buffalo, NY 14224

Portions of this work were originally authored by Dawn Titmus and published as *Reptiles and Amphibians*.
All new material this edition authored by Anne O'Daly.

Design Manager: Keith Davis
Picture Manager: Sophie Mortimer

Photo Credits:
Front Cover: Shutterstock: cynoclub br, Tawat Hantrakool tr, Eric Isselee bl, Olhastock tl.
Interior: Alamy: Milton Solomon 17t, Dreamstime: 9t, Cathy Keifer 11b; iStock: FOTOGRAFIA INC 13b, Grafner 15t, Courtney Hale 17b, kali9 12b, Mark Kostich 13t, loki1982 26, ross1248 1, 22, SerrNovik 4bl, Suwat Siriutcharungc 25b, Snowleopard1 27b, the4js 15b; Shutterstock: Alikosina 7c, Vladimir Bagnyuk 10-11, Blur Life 1975 8bl, Vince Bradley 19t, Brownyn Photo 21b, BW Folsom 8bc, Pei Chung Davy 29tl, Marta Cobos 8cl, cynoclub 6, Dobermaraner 20, Lukas Gojda 4-5, Tawat Hantrakool 4br, Eric Isselee 1c, 24, Andrey Janulin 7tr, Maria Jeffs 1r, Matt Jeppson 29b, JW Design 23b, D. Kucharski/L. Kucharska 25t, LagunaticPhoto 27t, Mehdi Photos 9br, Olga Moskvina 7cl, Nick Norman 9bl, obkung 16, Olhastock 5br, paytai 21t, Dmitry Petlin 18-19, picturepartners 7b, Ondrej Prosicky 14-15, reptiles4all 5, Swapan Photography 8bl, Wolfgang Simlinger 12r, Camilo Torres 23t, Tremor Photography 29t, Tsekhmister 1l, Marek Velechovsky 11t, werg 10, Melani Wright 19b, xpixel 8cr.
Key: t=top, b=bottom, c=center, l=left, r=right

Cataloging-in-Publication Data

Names: O'Daly, Anne
Title: Reptiles and amphibians / Anne O'Daly.
Description: Buffalo, New York : Kidhaven Publishing, 2024. |
Series: The coolest pets| Includes index and glossary
Identifiers: ISBN 9781534545380 (pbk) | ISBN 9781534545397 (library bound) | ISBN 9781534545403 (ebook)
Subjects: LCSH: Amphibians-- Juvenile literature | Amphibians as pets--Juvenile literature |
Pets--Juvenile literature | Reptiles--Juvenile literature | Reptiles as pets--Juvenile literature |
Classification: LCC SF459.R4 O33 2024 | DDC 639.3--dc23

Manufactured in the United States of America

CPSIA compliance information: Batch #CSKH24: For further information contact Greenhaven Publishing LLC at 1-844-317-7404.

Please visit our website, www.greenhavenpublishing.com.
For a free color catalog of all our high-quality books, call toll free 1-844-317-7404 or fax 1-844-317-7405.

Find us on

Contents

Choosing a Pet

Reptiles and amphibians are unusual but fascinating pets. There are lots to choose from, so you should choose the type that fits your family and its lifestyle.

How Long?

Many reptiles and amphibians have long lives. Some frogs can live for up to 15 years, some snakes up to 20 years or more, and some pet turtles for 50 years or more. Make sure you are prepared to look after your pet for as long as it lives!

Adopt a Pet

Rescue centers and shelters are full of pets that need new homes. Think about giving a pet from a rescue center a forever home. Rescue centers can also give advice about the best way to care for your new pet.

Checklist

- Can you provide a safe home for your pet?
- Do you have the space for a tank for your pet?
- Do you have the time to care for your pet every day over many years?
- Can your family afford the costs to buy the tank and food and pay vet bills?

Where to Buy

If you cannot find a pet at your local rescue center, buy one directly from a breeder or a good pet store. Check out notices for pets at the vet. Make sure you buy a healthy pet. Look for clear, bright eyes, and no discharge from the eyes, nose, or mouth.

Check the Law

Be sure to check your local laws. In some states, it's illegal to keep certain reptiles and amphibians as pets.

Next Steps

Reptiles and amphibians are awesome pets. They are less demanding than some pets, but it is important to choose the right one for you. This book tells you about six of the most popular types and shows you how to make a fun snake toy. You will also find some fascinating facts about your new friend!

Getting Started

Make sure you have everything you need before you bring your pet home. You will need equipment, including heating and lighting.

Setting Up the Tank

You will need a glass or plastic tank large enough for your pet. Reptiles and amphibians are cold-blooded—they need outside sources of heat to warm their bodies. Usually, you will need to heat the tank and keep the humidity at the right level. Use a thermometer to check the temperature and a gauge to check the humidity.

Checklist

- Tank large enough for your pet.
- Daylight lamp and heat bulb or heat mat.
- Lining material for the tank and hiding places.
- Food and water containers.
- Humidity gauge and thermometer.
- Small-animal keeper (for live food).
- Filter system, water heater, and water conditioner for aquatic turtles.

Lamps

Many captive reptiles and amphibians need special lighting over the tank to mimic daylight. This keeps them healthy. The daylight lamps should be left on for 10 to 12 hours a day.

Daylight lamp

Aquatic Pets

Aquatic turtles need water for swimming. Keep the water clean with a filter system and water conditioner. You will also need to use a water heater to keep the water at the correct temperature for your pet. Change the water about once a week to keep your pet healthy.

Live Food

Some pets such as lizards eat live food, including mealworms and crickets. If you keep the live food at home, you will need a secure enclosure for it. You will also need to give it food and water.

Mealworms

A Home for Your Pet

Knowing where your pet lives in the wild will help you set up its home. Your pet's housing should be as close to its natural habitat as possible.

Inside the Tank

Make sure your pet has somewhere to hide in the tank. Pets can get stressed if they do not have places to shelter. Artificial plants or bark help make your pet's home more natural.

Lining the Tank

Line the bottom of the tank with substrate, such as bark, moss, sand, or coconut fiber. Find out what type of material is best for your pet. Some pets like to burrow, so they will need a deep layer of substrate.

Coconut fiber

Bark

Moss

Sand

Lighting

Many reptiles and amphibians need 10 to 12 hours of daylight a day to stay healthy. Do not put their tank in direct sun. Instead, use special lighting over the tank that has ultraviolet A (UVA) and ultraviolet B (UVB) rays to mimic sunlight.

Humidity

Some reptiles and amphibians live in deserts in the wild and need a low level of humidity in the tank. Others need more humid conditions. Find out what humidity your pet prefers. Use a water sprayer to mist your pet's tank if it is too dry.

Water Sprayer

Aquatic Turtles

The tank for aquatic turtles should be big enough to hold 10 gallons (38 liters) of water for every inch (2.5 cm) of the turtle's length. Turtles need a warm, dry surface for basking and a ramp for climbing onto it. Use a light to heat the basking zone to the correct temperature for your pet. Put a cover on the tank to protect your turtle from other family pets.

Ramp

Food and Water

The kind of food your pet eats depends on which type of animal it is. Find out what food is best for your pet and how often you need to feed it.

Ready-Made

You can buy food made specially for your type of pet at the store. Bearded dragons, for example, need insects, vegetables, and fruit in their diet. You can buy pellets that contain everything they need to eat. Pet stores also sell pellets for turtles and iguanas.

Water

Your pet needs fresh water every day. Amphibians absorb water through their skin. Do not give your pet water straight from the faucet as it contains chemicals that can harm it. Use bottled spring water or water that has been treated to remove the chemicals and change it every day.

Food for Snakes

In the wild, snakes eat mammals, birds, amphibians, fish, and other reptiles. Feed a mouse to your adult pet snake every 7 to 10 days. You can buy frozen mice from pet stores or online. Make sure the mouse is thawed to room temperature first. Do not feed your pet snake live food. It may bite or injure your pet.

Eating Insects

Lizards, frogs, and salamanders eat a variety of insects. Many lizards like live food, such as crickets. Some lizards eat only plants. Some frogs eat locusts, cockroaches, and pinky mice. You may need to give your pet extra minerals and vitamin D. You can buy vitamin and mineral powder at the pet store.

Keeping Healthy

Good food and the right kind of home will help keep your pet healthy. If your pet does get ill, it's best to find a vet with experience in treating reptiles and amphibians.

Mites and Ticks

Mites and ticks can cause skin problems and spread diseases. Snake mites are usually black and are often found around the eyes. Lizard mites are red to orange. They hide in folds of skin or between the toes. Ticks are larger than mites. Take your pet to the vet if you see mites or ticks.

Fungus

Aquatic turtles can get fungus growing on their legs and in cracks in the shell. Amphibians can get fungal disease, too. Look for a white, cottonlike substance. It can be caused by dirty water or the tank being too humid. If your pet has fungus, take it to the vet.

Shedding Skin

Reptiles and amphibians shed their skin several times a year throughout their lives. Problems can occur with shedding if the tank is too dry. Spray it lightly with water to help your pet loosen the skin. Once your pet has finished shedding, remove the dead skin from the tank.

Signs of Sickness

- Your pet is not eating or drinking.
- It has swollen joints.
- It is hiding most of the time.
- It has runny eyes, nose, or mouth.
- Its droppings are runny for more than two days.
- It has lost weight.
- Its skin is discolored.

Take your pet to the vet if you think it may be sick.

Good Hygiene

Amphibians have delicate skin. Don't handle them unless you have to. If you handle your pet, wash your hands well afterward. Reptiles and amphibians carry bacteria, which can cause disease in humans. Clean the tank every two to three weeks and wear gloves when cleaning.

In the Wild

Many reptiles and amphibians live in warm places. But they can be found all over the world, apart from Antarctica. Most reptiles live on land, though some can live in the water. Amphibians live both on land and in water.

Lizards

Lizards live in most parts of the world, including the Americas from southern Canada to the southern tip of South America, Europe, most of Asia, Africa, and Australia. They usually live in warm climates, but some have adapted to live in cooler regions.

Amphibians

Usually, amphibians are animals that spend part of their life in water and part on land. Most young amphibians live in water and have gills to breathe, and the adults live on land. But some amphibians live entirely on land, and others spend their whole lives in water. Frogs, toads, caecilians, and salamanders are all amphibians.

Turtles and Tortoises

Turtles that live on land are called tortoises. Those that live in fresh water are aquatic turtles. Sea turtles live in the oceans, and terrapins live both on land and in water. There are more than 300 species of turtles and tortoises. They have four legs and a hard, protective shell made from bony plates. They live in deserts, tropical forests, and lakes on all the continents except Antarctica, and in seas all over the world.

Snakes

There are more than 3,200 different species of snakes. They live all over the world apart from polar regions, Iceland, Ireland, and New Zealand. Sea snakes live in all the oceans apart from the Atlantic Ocean. Snakes are more numerous in warm places.

Most snake species lay eggs, but those that live in cold places generally give birth to live young.

Red-eared Slider

The red-eared slider is a good pet for beginners. It is one of the most popular pet turtles, but it needs a large tank.

Where in the World?

The red-eared slider comes from the eastern United States and northern Mexico. It has been introduced to many areas of the world. It lives in slow-moving freshwater creeks, as well as in lakes and swamps. It is illegal in the United States to sell a turtle that has a shell less than 4 inches (10 cm) long.

The red-eared slider has red ear patches on its head.

Pet Care

Feed turtle pellets to your pet every other day. You can also give it dark, leafy greens, freeze-dried shrimp, and crickets. Feed your pet in a separate container so it does not make a mess in its tank.

* Use a heater to keep the water temperature at 75 to 85°F (24 to 29°C).
* Use a lamp to heat the basking area to 85 to 90°F (29 to 32°C). Also use a daylight lamp.

Profile

Red-eared sliders are semiaquatic turtles. They spend some time in water and other times basking on land in the wild. Their skin is green with yellow stripes. Adult red-eared sliders grow to about 12 inches (30 cm) long. Females are slightly larger than males. Red-eared sliders can live for more than 20 years.

Corn Snake

The corn snake is easy to handle. It makes a good family pet and is among the most popular pet snakes.

Where in the World?

In the wild, the corn snake lives in the eastern United States, north to New Jersey, and west into Utah and Colorado. It is often found in corn fields and corn supplies, which is how it got its name.

Corn snakes can become quite tame.

Pet Care

The corn snake needs a tank that is at least 20 gallons (78 liters) with an escape-proof lid. Provide hide boxes, such as PVC pipe or a hollow log, and branches for climbing.

- Feed your pet freshly killed or frozen and thawed rodents every 7 to 10 days.
- Use a heat pad or light to create a warm zone of 85°F (29°C). The cool zone should be in the low 70s°F (20s°C).

Profile

The corn snake is orange to red-brown and comes in a range of patterns. In the wild, they live mostly on the ground, but they also like to climb. Adults grow to 4 to 6 feet (1.2 to 1.8 m) long. Pet corn snakes can live from 12 to 20 years.

Leopard Gecko

Leopard geckos are friendly and curious. They are usually easy to handle and make excellent pets for first-time owners.

The leopard gecko stores fat in its long tail.

Where in the World?

The leopard gecko comes from Afghanistan, Iraq, Iran, northwest India, and Pakistan in South Asia. In the wild, it lives in dry and semidry desert regions and grasslands.

Pet Care

House your pet in a 10- or 20-gallon (38 or 78 liter) tank and provide it with hide boxes.

- Feed your pet live food such as crickets every other day. Dust the food with vitamin and mineral powder every other feed.
- Heat a basking zone to 87 to 90°F (30 to 32°C). The cool zone can be 74 to 80°F (23 to 27°C).

Profile

The leopard gecko gets its name from its yellow skin covered with brown stripes or spots, which looks like leopard skin. Adults grow 8 to 10 inches (20 to 25 cm) in length. Males are larger than females. Leopard geckos are nocturnal and are rarely seen during the day. They can usually live for 8 to 10 years, but sometimes live as long as 20 years.

Bearded Dragon

This lizard has a collar of spines around its neck. If a bearded dragon feels threatened, it can make its spines stand up.

Where in the World?

The bearded dragon comes from central and eastern Australia. It lives in deserts, dry forests, and scrublands.

Pet Care

House your pet in a tank with hide boxes, logs for it to climb on, and a dish of water large enough for it to bathe in.

- Use a lamp to heat the basking zone to 95 to 110°F (35° to 43°C). Also use a daylight lamp.
- Feed your pet live food, such as crickets, four or five times a week. Also feed it chopped vegetables and fruit. Dust the food with calcium and vitamin powder once a week.

Profile

The bearded dragon has a triangular head and spiny scales on its body. Its color can be brown, tan, gray, green, orange, or red. Adults can grow up to 2 feet (60 cm) long, including the tail. Bearded dragons can become quite tame and will feed from their keeper's hand. They usually live for 7 to 10 years.

Pacman Frog

The Pacman frog is a good beginner pet. It is easy to care for, but doesn't like to be handled.

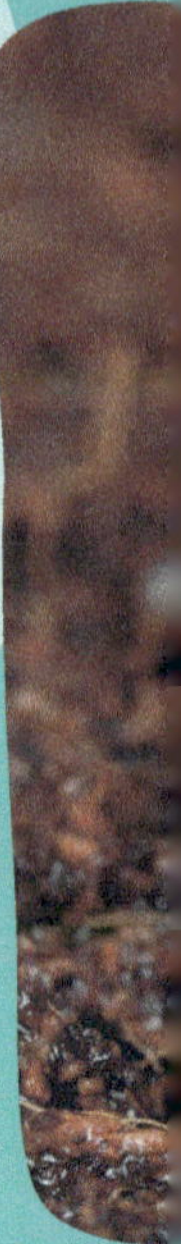

The Pacman frog gets its name from a video game character that had a large mouth and big appetite!

Where in the World?

The Pacman frog lives in Argentina, Uruguay, and southern Brazil in South America. It lives near freshwater marshes and pools in forests. It is also called the Argentine or ornate horned frog.

Pet Care

House your pet in a 10-gallon (38 L) tank lined with damp material such as coconut fiber. Give it fresh, clean water every day.

* Heat the tank to 75 to 82°F (24 to 28°C).
* Feed your adult pet about once a week. It eats earthworms, locusts, cockroaches, crickets, and mice. Do not handle your pet–it may bite!

Profile

The Pacman frog has a large mouth and hornlike upper lids above its eyes. It comes in a range of colors, including yellow, green, orange, and brown. Females usually grow 4 to 6 inches (10 to 15 cm) long. Males are smaller. They are usually almost as wide as their length. Pacman frogs can live up to 10 years.

Tiger Salamander

The tiger salamander is a fun pet. It can learn to recognize its keeper and "ask" for food! It has sensitive skin so it must be handled with care.

The tiger salamander is named for its striped markings.

Where in the World?

There are several closely related species of tiger salamanders. They are found throughout the United States, as well as in southern Canada and northern Mexico. In some states, it is illegal to own a tiger salamander. Check the laws in your state before you buy this pet.

Pet Care

Tiger salamanders like to burrow. Line the tank with a deep layer of substrate such as coconut fiber. Keep the substrate damp in half the tank.

* Feed your pet live crickets, earthworms, and cockroaches two to three times a week.
* There is no need to use special lighting or to heat the tank. A temperature of about 70°F (21°C) or lower is fine for your pet.

Profile

Tiger salamanders can be olive green, black, or yellow with brown, black, yellow, or gray markings. They have a rounded snout with an upturned mouth that makes them look like they are smiling! They grow up to 6 to 13 inches (15 to 33 cm) long. They can live between 15 and 20 years.

Easy-to-Make

Slithery Snake

Make a cute snake from some egg cartons and paint it any color you like. Pull it along the floor to make it slither.

You Will Need:

- Cardboard egg carton
- Scissors
- Tempera paint in two or more colors
- Paintbrush
- Yarn or string
- Red construction paper
- Glue
- Wiggle eyes

1 Cut out six cups from the egg carton. Cut off any ragged tops.

2 Paint the cups in two or more different colors inside and out. Or you could paint the cups in one color and add stripes or spots in another color. Let the paint dry.

3 Arrange the cups in a line. Stand the head on its side so the open side faces forward.

4 Ask an adult to make small holes on either side of the five body cups. Make one hole in the head cup.

5 Push a long piece of string or yarn through the holes to tie the cups together. Tie a knot inside the head. Leave a length of yarn or string so you can pull your snake along.

6 Cut a forked tongue shape from the construction paper and glue it to the inside of the head. Glue two wiggle eyes on top of the head.

Fun Facts

The largest turtle in the world is the leatherback sea turtle. It can grow up to 8 feet (2.4 m) in length.

The fire salamander has large poison glands on its body. It can squirt poison at prey from glands on its back.

Mexican beaded lizards and Gila monsters are lizards that kill their prey using poison in their saliva.

There are more than 10,000 reptile species and more than 7,700 amphibian species.

Some toads, such as the female Surinam toad, carry their eggs on their back until they hatch. The male midwife toad carries the eggs glued to his legs.

The Aldabra giant tortoise can live for 150 years or more. A male called Jonathan is thought to be the oldest living tortoise in the world. It is thought he hatched in 1832.

Most snakes have brown or black coloring that blends in with their surroundings. However, some snakes are highly colored. The bright colors of the coral snake warn predators not to attack.

The tuatara is a type of reptile found only on small islands off the coast of New Zealand. They can live for 100 years or more.

Glossary

burrow make a tunnel or hole in the ground by digging.

fungus (plural, fungi) type of simple life-form, such as mold. Some fungi can cause disease.

gland organ in the body that produces a substance, such as sweat.

habitat place an animal or plant naturally lives.

humidity amount of moisture in the air.

iguana large lizard that lives in Central and South America.

mealworm young form of a beetle, often used as pet food.

mimic create the effect of something.

mineral substance found in food that is important for good health.

mite very small animal that lives on plants, animals, and food.

pellet small, hard ball of food for animals.

pinky mouse young mouse without fur.

predator animal that kills other animals for food.

saliva liquid produced in the mouth.

scrubland area with small bushes and trees.

substrate layer of material that lines the bottom of a tank.

tick very small insect that attaches itself to a larger animal and feeds on it.

ultraviolet (UV) describes light rays found in sunlight that cannot be seen.

vitamin D natural substance that is important for healthy bones, found in some foods and created by exposure to sunlight.

water conditioner substance used to remove harmful chemicals from water.

Further Resources

Books

Clasky, Leonard. *Let's Tell Jokes About Snakes.* New York, NY: Windmill Books, 2023.

Rossiter, Brienna. *My Pet Snake.* Mendota Heights, MN: Little Blue Readers, 2023.

Shea, Therese M. *Is a Turtle a Good Pet for Me?* New York, NY: PowerKids Press, 2020.

Websites

All About Snakes
easyscienceforkids.com/all-about-snakes/
Explore more fun facts about snakes.

10 Totally Awesome Facts About Turtles!
www.natgeokids.com/uk/discover/animals/sea-life/turtle-facts/
Discover more terrific turtle facts, especially if you're interested in keeping one as a pet!

Snakes
www.dkfindout.com/us/animals-and-nature/reptiles/snakes/
Interested in having a snake as a pet? Read more about these slithering reptiles.

Publisher's note to parents and teachers: Our editors have reviewed the websites listed here to make sure they're suitable for students. However, websites may change frequently. Please note that students should always be supervised when they access the internet.

Index